Lamentations

Lamentations

GEORGE FRANKLIN

The poems in this volume have previously
appeared in the following publications:

"Lot's Lament": *Roof: An Anthology of Poetry from the
Naropa Institute.* Boulder, Colorado: Summer, 1976.

"Elegy in Broken Stanzas": *Contour with Shadow.*
Brooklyn, New York: The Frolic Press, 2017.

"Talking Head": *ep;phany, a literary journal.*
New York, New York: Winter/Spring, 2009.

"Via Dolorosa": *Contour with Shadow.*
Brooklyn, New York: The Frolic Press, 2017.

"The Frame": *The Recorder: The Journal of the
American Irish Historical Society.*

For permission requests, write to the publisher
through their website at ristrettobooks.org

Paperback ISBN: 979-8-9882429-6-3

Ebook ISBN:979-8-9882429-7-0

for Jeffrey Gustavson

Contents

❖

I

Lot's Lament

Because I could not see what she saw,
I invented the burning city that gives no heat,
I planted the pillar of salt that is no resource,
And now, as their shadows wave at my feet,
I imagine the horrified look she gave
And salvage her look that has turned from me.
I almost forgot the pillar, the unfinished temple,
My marriage to impossibility: I keep finding
The face that abandons me: still turning,
Too violent and rapid to feel,
Like colors that blend on a spinning wheel
Whose motion I neither inspire nor postpone.
I want to wear her, to wear her out,
But my face is no more expressive than stone.
Though it shatter me, I must break within
Where she stares beneath my forehead's drawn skin,
Toward the mended vision reversed past my eyes,
Toward a law I cannot recognize,
To the haven where I am accused and disowned,
Where the wheel is stopped and I break apart
Into colors that I have never known.

Elegy in Broken Stanzas

I was an aristocratic boy, you
            were an aristocratic boy,
At a time when that moniker was as much a mark
Of odium as of rank,

When all loudly proclaimed an equal birthright—
            although ours, as unwilling avatars
Of a hegemony on the wane,
Was increasingly derided, disdained.

And so you and I, scions of parallel lines,
                        suppressed all signs
Of our dubious provenance.
Still, what we concealed from our confederates

Remained transparent to each other;
            an affinity, sealed by no word
Of acknowledgment, bound us lightly together
In a tacit co-conspiracy of two.

And yet you alone, as though by divine right,
                        primus inter pares,
Presided, nonchalant, over a meritocracy of genes
(Or so we believed) not genealogy.

Turning inward, we turned our backs
            on our too-studious brethren,

On the teleologically self-driven, the dull careerists
Rehearsing rote roles in life's play.

Insouciance, wit, intelligence, beauty—
These were the qualities, neither means nor ends,
                    that we chose to cultivate
And for which we were scorned,

Indicted as pretentious, as poseurs,
        castigated by stolid elders
Who regarded us as mere profligates or wastrels
Squandering our talents, our days.

But we, in turn, spoke another language;
                    our words, like artifacts,
Unlike coins—the hard currency, endlessly
Reproduced, valued by our fathers—

Were exchanged in an economy of cherished
        and reciprocated gifts, free, open-ended,
In which each participant was enriched
By the enrichment of all.

And some of us, yes, assayed poems,
                    circulated in the same
Spirit, seeking approbation from each other,
Only later, perhaps, from wider circles

That might come to celebrate our names;
        but still, for now, we remained
Each other's patrons, each other's exemplary
Audience, fit though few.

When we gathered in sunlit courtyards
                    or lingered over dinners
At which wine abundantly flowed, our banter,
Our thrust and parry, like most games,

Was far from entirely unserious;
            though careful to appear casual players,
We manically strove to outdo each other;
Still, we were content, magnanimous

Even in defeat, our shared laughter
                    revealing that we contended
As one, partners in an enterprise and an ethos
In which we all claimed a stake.

Yet how often, my friend, you stood out
            amidst our revels, sometimes their instigator,
Sometimes their audience, but always
The center of our attention,

Shining both inwardly and outwardly,
                    your slightest gesture
Imbued with grace, your lively face
Reflecting each nuance of our figured speech.

Your body slender, strong,
            long-limbed, your torso flaring upward
From your narrow waist, your mind, too, athletic—
Your repartee outstripped our own.

How ardently we, your devotees,
                    responded to every cue,
Verbal or nonverbal, you sowed among us,
Seducing, enthralling us, engendering,

Through no apparent effort
          or edict of will, the life of our little Eden
That seemed to be formed in your sovereign image,
Our idolatry only partly disguised

By our feigned diffidence—
                    our refusal to appear
Childishly credulous, to regard ourselves,
Sophisticates, as constituents of a cult.

Many to whom you granted audience,
          both male and female, though aware
You were already spoken for, imagined themselves
Your privileged paramour.

In our reveries each was your one and only
                    not merely one of many,
A fantasy we knew would never be realized
However sweet it was to entertain.

How well I remember the night
          when one of your male votaries,
Having imbibed to excess (no, far beyond excess),
Begged you to return with him

To his rooms and presumably
                    to his narrow bed,
And how you replied that but for societal mores
You would have happily complied.

It struck me, whether your words
        were, in fact, *true*—and I more than suspected
They were not—that they constituted
A brilliantly improvised act

Of compassion, clear and uncompromising,
                        rescuing one of our tribe
From what would otherwise have registered
As an unpardonable gaucherie,

Not merely an embarrassment
        but a cruel humiliation
That might have shattered him, occasioning
A catastrophic loss of face.

Your reply itself entailed, of course,
                        a conspicuous breach
Of those very, apparently unequivocal, mores
That you claimed constrained you,

Challenging them with a fine irony
        while boldly risking loss of status, the sacrifice
Of your cock-of-the-walk prestige,
To uphold the dignity of a brother.

That night you became,
                as did our little coterie,
More real to me, as though a mask had been lifted,
Revealing the human face beneath.

I remembered how days before
        you had waved an opened envelope before us,
And had laughingly extracted from it
A page mysteriously blank.

My devoted father, you intoned,
                    dutifully sends
Me a letter, punctually, every month, knowing
How vital it is that we keep in touch.

We all laughed with you,
            as usual, but I was stunned by the ruthless,
Reptilian cruelty of that non-letter,
By its intent to insult and summarily dismiss.

I laughed, too, of course, reflexively
                    eliding a pain,
Your pain, that I could only surmise, and was unable
Either to acknowledge or assuage.

I no longer regarded what remained
            unspoken between us
As a pact mutually chosen, but as a silence
Enforced by a code not our own,

And I felt a closeness to you
                    deeper, more intense
Than the occult bonds of culture or caste,
An intimacy that I longed to confess.

But we were barely acquaintances,
            not friends. Outside of our shared circle
We had exchanged only a few desultory words
And I was too shy to seek you out.

And so I was pleasantly surprised
                    when a fellow poet,
Your girlfriend, invited me, another girl, and you
To spend a weekend at her parents' villa,

Perched precariously upon a high bluff
        that steeply sloped down to the sea.
On the evening of our arrival our hostess fell ill,
Withdrew with her friend to her room.

Settled in my own, I watched an heraldic sun
                        swell as it descended,
Crossing the horizon as the sea, the sky,
Flared scarlet, then faded. Later,

You and I walked down to the beach,
        To roiling surf that advanced and retreated
With a full-throated roar, its breaking crests
Illumined by a full moon.

You stripped off your clothes.
                        I followed your lead,
And then we were both running naked
On fine-grained sand that had been pummeled

By the perpetually grinding ocean.
    How glorious it felt, then,
To be in young bodies energized by the sea
That was itself persuaded by the pull of the moon

That shone down on us both,
                        its power
Felt in our blood as we breathed in and out,
Attuned to the waves that broke at our feet.

We ran a mile out and back,
        sprinting toward the end, crossing

An invisible finish line at the same moment,
Doubling over with laughter and fatigue.

Racing chest high into currents that threatened
                                        to submerge us,
We held fast, our hands slapping rough water,
Dousing each other with spray,

Then lay side by side on the sand,
            you gazing at the moon, I glancing at you,
Furtively admiring the perfect lines of your body,
Contours silvered by rays they made visible.

My senses heightened, my mind dazed,
                              I do not know
How long we stayed there, but I do remember
Feeling torn, paralyzed in the moment,

Both wanting and not wanting to touch
            or be touched by you, wishing
That we could remain suspended there forever,
Lying in tandem beneath a limitless sky.

Eventually, of course, you got up,
                              draped a towel
Around your waist, and headed for the house.
I lingered for a while, unwilling to break

A spell that had already been broken.
            Later I, too, arose,
Feeling unaccountably sad, diminished,
As though I'd failed a test impossible to pass.

When I opened the door to the house
                    I saw you still naked,
Supine on the floor, your girlfriend's friend
Bending over your hips, providing

A service that startled, embarrassed me.
          Pretending to have seen nothing,
I bolted to my room, lay on my bed. I knew
That you were neither callous

Nor careless of my feelings
                    and so pondered
The purport of the tableau vivant
Upon which I had almost comically stumbled.

Perhaps you were letting me know,
          if unconsciously, that had *I* made a move
It would have been me bending over you,
A scenario I might have desired

But could never have embraced
                    unless it had entailed
The explicit avowal of an inviolate bond,
A betrothal of body and spirit

That I knew was not fated for us;
          or perhaps I was simply
Fearful of the act itself, of an intensity in which
I might lose myself. Still hoping to be found,

When I returned to our cherished circle,
                    its epoch a blessed
Interregnum, an interstitial time never destined
To indefinitely last, I understood

That I could no longer inhabit it,
      At least not fully, unreservedly, and
so I attended its gatherings less and less
Until, hardly noticing, I stopped returning at all.

After that, my friend, I scarcely
                encountered you,
Although I remained grateful for the spaces,
However fraught, you had disclosed within me.

I was an aristocratic boy,
      you were an aristocratic boy;
We strove, each in his way, for a nobility of spirit,
A standard I, at least, never quite attained.

Eventually our little group dispersed,
                an inevitable diaspora.
Some, I heard, kept in touch, even organized
A few raucous, high-spirited reunions;

Most, of course, abandoning poetry,
      became conspicuously
Solid citizens with solid professions
And with family circles supported by their toils.

Though never quite relinquishing the mores
              of our golden cenacle,
I spurned the overtures of my former comrades,
Refusing to face all reminders of loss.

My life grew liminal, vexed, covert,
      relegated to the margins
Of worlds in which, never outgrowing the boy
I once was, still subject to his fears, desires,

Ambitions, I could never feel at home.
                              I labored at my verses
But no longer gladly anticipated an immediate
Response, discerning and sympathetic;

Instead my good works were entrusted
                    to my own purview, to an audience of one,
Becoming increasingly hermetic,
Dead to a world in which they had no place.

I kept seeking, my friend, but never met
                              a chosen other in whom
I might lose and find myself—a fruitless ideal
That my love for you had led me to envisage.

It was as though I kept approaching
                    a threshold that kept receding
Or vanishing as I grew near, impossible to cross—
Or perhaps, again, I was fearful of crossing it;

Perhaps I unwittingly chose the sole,
                              habitually estranged self
That possessed me, feeling increasingly unreal,
Unreachable, unredeemable, cut off

From the vibrant energy of life itself,
          the wellsprings of grace from which
We once drank, not knowing how lucky we were
Or that they could ever dry up.

Decades later, I am in irrevocable exile.
                    Our brief time together
Feels like ancient history, unchronicled, effaced,
Living only in the shadow house of memory.

Insouciance, wit, intelligence, beauty—
        all have now thoroughly deserted me.
Specters of *age, pain, despondency, madness*
Are my constant, unwanted companions.

Each morning, my friend, it is as though
              I receive an envelope,
Must extract a page upon which no characters
Appear, upon which I can no longer write

Either poems or the barest outline
        of some new chapter of a life
That now feels effectively over, yet refuses,
Adamantly, to relinquish me,

A page that remains as empty
            as these leaden hours
That seem to last forever, tending nowhere,
Toward no imaginable, redemptive end.

My will exhausted, I can feel nothing
        but terror and the terror of nothingness;
Whatever word or image arises in my mind
Prompts only a scalding regret.

Yet sometimes I struggle to hold to the notion
            that the whole of a life
Cannot be judged by any one segment of it,
That its end is no more definitive

Than all that has preceded it,
        that my life has been not only a catalogue
Of errors leading to an intolerable impasse,
That I have performed some acts of dignity, of worth.

And, if time, though felt by us as diachronic,
                    is also synchronic
And can be spread out before us like a map
After we cross life's final threshold,

Then somewhere still our little group
        is reconvening, its members all young again,
Laughing, remonstrating with each other,
Their lives lying before them;

Then somewhere, my friend, you are still
                    suavely holding court,
Exchanging ripostes with the best of us, or saving,
With a fine generosity, a friend from himself;

Somewhere still we are running exultantly
        on a beach at night, reveling
In our bodies' impossible freedom, not thinking
Beyond ourselves, not thinking at all,

Merely listening, hypnotized, to waves
                    surging and retreating,
Their emphatic pulse commingling ecstatically
With the rhythms of our breath and blood;

Still, still we are plunging into the sea,
        waters from which we rise naked, restored,
Recovering a moment, endlessly suspended, in which
We lie together beneath a blazing sky.

II

Talking Head

for Sheila

So many words have been put into my mouth
It's a wonder I've any left to call my own;
I mean those dreary rehearsals, poem after poem,
Of things that never happened, not to me—
Of my tragic, uxorious love for Eurydice,
Of my pitiful rescue mission, traffic with shades,
Of my foolish bargain with the Lord of Hell.
Well, when I look back, my agonized recollection
Is not of some dream of what could not have been
Dispelled by the cold light of sobering day;
My affections had always bent the other way.
Are we all reduced to our legends in the end?
I never *had* a consort. Playing solo
Was all I'd done, all I'd been chosen to do.
Apollo sired me, bequeathed me my lyre,
Ordained me as a priest of Dionysus,
To temper his savagery with my tremulous lays.
God, how I rue that summons, and that day!

It was D, of course, who had a knack for girls,
Outlandish rock star, face a mask, mere show,
His act all hollow percussion, driving beat.
It was he who started underground, made it big,
Emerged as from some source enticingly foreign,
Tossed on our white sands as by the sea,
A metaphor his crazed fans took literally—

Thus that lurid, odd, biennial argosy,
Their idol wheeled, shore to city, in a ship,
A painted prop, too fragile for any wave,
While they raved loud around him, a procession
Graced, too, by loutish goatboys wielding dildos,
Chanting his lewd dithyrambs, his punk anthems,
His solemn rite turned plain obscenity;
The advent of their hero—precious captive!—
Roused a mock greeting fit for a pilfered slave
Who slipped away, and headed for the hills,
Their capsized hearts left seized yet dispossessed,
By his daft abandon ravaged and enthralled.

His every appearance sparked the same sensation
That quickly spread, a sickening conflagration,
An epidemic—no, a plague, whose fever
Its victims gladly caught, and, mad, passed on.
Androgyne stroking his phallus and his tresses,
He teased our decorous virgins to a frenzy
Until they lost themselves and ran in packs,
Groupies, harpies, furies, fates, Maenads,
Relentlessly tracking down that thing they loved,
Could never get enough of, like a drug
Whose simulated ecstasy trumped bright day.
And he, poor fool, could not, dared not control
The very force that he himself unleashed,
But threw his effigies into their roiling mosh pit
(Bulls, suckling calves, goats, lions, snakes—
How many bestial forms he wore and sloughed!)
Where they were torn, predictably, limb from limb,
The raw meat of his barbarous communion:
A god both of destruction and self-destruction,
The fate he feigned augmented his fatal allure.

Blood brother to the dancing God, Lord Shiva,
(Ecstatic one who drank from the cosmic sea
The whole world's poison, transmuted it within—
Fierce alchemist whose crucible was himself—
To a quintessential nectar, and so survived,
His omnipotent *lingam* stirring in every *yoni*,
Lord both of death and conquering life, revived)
My wayward charge could never truly die.

Imagine the dreadful license exemption bred!
It was he, and he alone, who had compacted
With hell, disreputable mineshaft, and its Lord
And with his promiscuous father, god of gods,
As indulgent with his son as with himself;
Together, axial poles of the turning world,
They conspired, ever faithful, to secrete him,
Below, above, but safely out of bounds,
His limbs reknit, rebaptized in lake or sea,
Until, again, the earth quaked. Bromios roared
The blessing of his catastrophic word,
Braying his senseless name at the full moon
As, perched upon a high crag shagged by clouds,
A stream of golden light poured from his jaws,
Glowing like lava from some fresh eruption—
Prodigious prodigal that night adored.
Mysterium tremens! Their god's epiphany
Sent thrills of delirium through his votaries,
Expectant, who awaited his plighted return,
Yearning for their dance to begin yet again,
For their revels' entrancing, orgiastic rout.

Like his pale precursors, Osiris, Attis, Adonis,
The boy who never grows up kept showing up,

Forever unattainable, forever drawing near,
Still vacant behind the mask of his dazzling enigma,
Breaking the hearts of those who would be broken
Like him, yet live to break another day.
Like Elvis, worshiped at his shrine in Memphis,
Dionysus was ever a mama's boy at heart;
How he pined for Semele, his lost mortal part,
Vaporized by one bolt from a jealous father!
An aborted thing, snatched from her still-hot ashes,
Peremptorily stitched into the god's hard thigh,
This cramped gestation yielded a second birth
Unnatural, unlaborious, still premature—
A tale to arouse any virgin's pity and scorn,
Inciting emotions half-sexual, half-maternal
(An uneasy concatenation of roles at best).
And so at each least Dionysus-sighting
His devotees, convulsed, quit hearth and home,
Eloping to high wastes of snow-capped mountains,
Hair streaming, suckling wild calves at their breasts
While panting shrill cries anything but maternal
To the Corybantic clash of clanging cymbals
Until, swayed by an instinct blind within them,
They conveyed their charges, then their god himself,
Safe to the font, to the womb of life or death.

Dreamed consummation, then tragic dispersal—
(A mess of limbs appalled their opening eyes)
Made worse by their implication in his demise,
A guilt that tore their world, rendered more telling
Their longing for his form, his fate's reprise,
As though his absence magnified his presence,
His death wore his more urgent life's disguise.

D, of course, kept laughing behind the scenes;
Through him the tragic turned toward the absurd—
Lord knows, at the close of a long, hard day
There's nothing quite like a rollicking satyr play!

No mere shape-shifter, he switched others' shapes,
Rearranging and deranging their forms and fates
With more than a director's or a dramatist's skill;
The whole world was the stage, or the blank screen
On which he worked his magic, his special effects,
His miracles, his mise-en-scène, his Maya,
Or, assuming the actor's role, directed himself
(Above all, he loved to see himself being seen)
With special care to entrances, quick exits
So stunning his fellow actors blew their lines.
But D alone truly *lived*, disappeared in his roles,
Agent as well as actor, pained sufferer, too,
And in his masques the illusory and the real
Converged, with not a jot of space between them.

Zagreus constantly slain, D ever reborn,
And Bromios faithfully bellowing at His side—
His names were like concurrent incarnations,
Lines warping through an unparalleled universe;
Cropping up here, there, everywhere, and nowhere,
He seemed to play no part, yet played them all.
And so, crude tyrant, martyred liberator,
He came as a stranger, conquering foreign lands
Of which, in truth, he'd always been a native,
Possessing, repossessing hearts and minds
He blessed and blasted, plagued and glibly saved,
Brave exile reclaiming polis after polis,
Confounding their too-rigorous paradigms.

He came from India, Persia, Arabia, Thrace,
His face in ruddy makeup, dread God of War,
After first tracing the same route in reverse
(A procession after which Lord Alexander,
Whose bent, ambivalent heart stiffened his will,
Would later style his straight, triumphal race).
A tempestuous male diva wreaking mayhem—
At once jack-booted vandal and femme fatale—
Upon his cowed, sycophantic retinue
Of would-be satyrs, aging boys in the band,
D imagined slights, exacted tribute due
To a demigod jealous of his name and fame,
His least or latest whim momentous law.

Such rumored antics proved a surefire draw.
This Generalissimo took each city by storm—
Heil promised *Ubermensch! Heil Zarathustra!*
His feral, high-pitched, vaunting rhetoric
Buckled the sold-out stadiums on his tour;
All clamored to greet his strobe-lit apparition;
After years of anticipation, the throes of release
Convulsed his throng, a wild, protracted labor,
An hysterical pregnancy issuing in no birth;
Some fainted, prostrate at his prancing feet,
While others jerked in spasms, jammed the aisles;
Still others froze, chills running up their spines,
Feared the crumbling temple would succumb,
Interring all beneath a spoiled brat's crown.

D saved his proudest gig for his home town.
Bandying lines with his dimwitted cousin,
A heart he'd hardened, blinded in advance,
He played an effeminate herald, a fey Hermes,
A hippie longhair whose guru's seductions

Corrupted matrons' morals, drove them wild
With Eastern notions (peace, love, back to nature).
What gall! He insisted Pentheus join the cult,
An insult framed to engender a fierce reply
The frantic, dumb-struck king failed to supply.

What better time to conjure a blind seer?
Tiresias knew which way the wind was blowing
(For him it used to blow both ways at once)
And so it was no great stretch to don a gown,
But Cadmus, too, was quick to ape the hipster;
Each young/old, male/female, neither/either.
These two, united, formed a winsome couple
As hand in hand they shuffled out of town.

How coyly, passively D accepted the shackles,
The cuffs by which he eagerly was bound,
A masked tyrant queerly glad to play the slave,
Like a smug dominant acting the submissive
In the practiced, lascivious choreography
Of some choice, preauthorized rite of S&M,
A game not to be tried with rougher trade,
But in the right hands an enthralling masquerade—

Only to break free! More fleet than Houdini,
He performed his miraculous magic in no time flat,
Was almost as quick to level the whole polis;
Its palace, temple, walls—all toppled down;
At the apex of the sole façade left standing
He gleefully pegged Pentheus' headless crown.

His act, of course, was not confined to land.
For D, the wine-dark sea was floating theater,
A protean stage for his outstanding pranks.

And so, a fetching youth, his comely feet
Printing the untrammeled sands of an ivory shore,
Soft zephyrs combing, uncombing his gold hair,
He caught the eyes of pirates, only too happy
After years of celibate toil, uncertain pay,
To ensnare, as sweetest spoil, such easy prey;
They stashed their trophy deep in the ship's hold.
But D, as ever, proved *himself* the pirate
As sprouts of profligate life spread everywhere;
Tendrils of ivy clutched the bellying sails
While thick vines snagged the oarlocks and the oars;
Wine, as though poured freely, but from no jars,
Exhaled its dank perfume, and kept on rising
Until it sloshed about the sailors' thighs;
A lion roared in the bow; in the stern a bear
Unbaited crammed its maw with human flesh.
A basilisk wound about the stiff mast, miming
The serpent-twins entwined round Hermes' staff
Or Moses' miraculous sign raised in the desert,
His rod-serpent-rod that with a salient tap
Released life-giving streams from penitent rock.
But D was a prophet of a different stripe—
The ship, enchanted vineyard, uncanny garden,
Would yield no promised land to its lost crew;
Sated, his sweet revenge almost complete,
In a grand deus ex machina, his ultimate coup,
He burst, glad day, in glory from the hold,
His wine, mixing with blood, soaking the planks,
And boldly seized the tiller, giving thanks
As his black vessel cut through cresting waves
That danced about it, in proud tumult raved.

Intimate with earth's depths as with high seas,
It was D, some said, at Demeter's behest,

Who descended, on cue, to rescue Persephone,
Hell's Queen, his second mother, virgin bride,
Abandoning her to the tender fields of spring.
It was he, nocturnal one, who burst the bonds
Of his ravenous hell hounds, the fell Erinyes,
Insatiable as the fiercest of Maenads,
Pouring through the earth's wide-yawning maw.
Requiting crimes that D himself incited,
Their vengeance, too, was its own sovereign law;
He summoned, from below, the riddling Sphinx,
Half woman, half lynx, devourer of men,
Sibyl reciting the lines of his cryptic script
(Rendering all but Oedipus stupefied and mute)
As a special prize to bedevil his closest kin—
Like death, no respecter of lineage, caste, or clan;
Thebes early had suffered his unfounded rage,
The keen stripes of his avid fennel whip.

Hades and Dionysus are one and the same,
Heraclitus, sage of paradox, proclaimed,
Who knew that *the way up is the way down.*
If not the same, then constantly trading places
In one of D's alternate self-mythologies,
Confederate, they harried uprooted shades
Who, shielding lidless eyes from the sun's rays,
Gadded about unhallowed on D's festal days—
For him yet one more play within his play.

All this was his force that I was bid to curb
Who could not help but feel his pervading charm;
I was, after all, his sworn priest, although bound
By a firm command to keep him within bounds.
O, endless indenture to a double bind—
I felt myself, day by day, growing more like him

Whom I was impossibly charged to civilize;
I sensed a fate like his growing within me,
Sensed, too, my own would be far more unkind.
My single father was no match for his
Dual-patron parentage, Olympian Zeus and Hades,
Lords of unspeakable heights, fathomless depths
I was taught to neither ponder nor traverse;
My melodious voice was trained to a middle range,
A golden mean, whole numbers, undistorted,
To chant of things familiar, not estranged;
But now I could faintly hear odd notes within me,
Dark intimations, brief, of a dissonance,
That later would surge up, and then submerge me,
Would be my portion in life's troubled dance.

Before that cruel, humiliating summons
To play priest, apologist, publicist to a phantom,
I had my own, my youthful golden time.
Uneducated in the world's deceptions,
My heart was almost as true as my perfect pitch.
I poured out my songs to the spontaneous pulse
That spoke within me, deftly plucked the strings
Whose resonance was the thrum of life itself;
And then I let my sweet words come unbidden—
No hunter, I had no need to track them down.

I seemed to move within a column of light
Whose radiance spread about me everywhere.
My senses, quick, engrossed their several objects
Not serially, yet distinctly—O, all at once
They vanished, reappeared in that golden shaft
Expanding, contracting, humming with such speed
It seemed to annul all sense of time itself
And so not to move at all, still standing fast

Like Zeno's arrow, staying while it flew.
And yet my song's circumference grew wider;
Tall sentinel trees bent toward it, and wild beasts,
Quitting their lairs, grew tame within my sight,
Breathed softy as I stroked my lyre's strings—

Yes, like a virgin's fingers working her loom
Within her father's house, weaving, unweaving,
Suspending, prolonging the day with her reverie,
Dreaming (half hoping, half dreading) the hour
When a youth bold as Hector, fair as Hyacinth
Would cross her threshold, steal her heart away:

So I, too, played within my father's house,
Its dome the sky, its boundary the horizon,
The unmarked line he broached in his flaring robes,
Twice daily trespassing, touching earth's domain
That he, its prince, had long since made his own;
He kept his distance, yet kept drawing near,
Or seemed to, when, alone, I chanted his name
And meted out my measures in strict song.
I kept to my proper rooms within his mansion,
Oak-vaulted vales where, carelessly, I wandered
And listened to blithe fish plash in the streams,
The bobcat purr, fleet insects whir midair,
Paired doves coo, and the falcon, wheeling, cry,
My only fear the gross shriek of Pan's pipe,
Twin organs fashioned from a nymph he raped
When came pillaging from his mountain lair,
Fanning quick panic through my reverent glades,
A priapic interlude far from mere comic relief;
Like one of D's cleft satyrs, half man, half goat,
Coward, he skulked back to his sullen rocks
While I renewed the hiatus of my vows.

I hymned a living sum, a breathing cosmos,
The whole in each part, each part in the whole
Addressed to every other in just proportion,
In numbers that my instinctive octave sounded
And sounding, did its own part to uphold.
The stars and planets spinning in their courses,
Each root, trunk, branch, leaf, and winding vein
That flourished beneath the slow arc of the sun,
The rainbow parsing its colors in bright mist,
Constraining banks permitting streams to flow,
All spoke to my eyes a proximate symmetry;
O, only by being bounded were things free
To open outward toward light's unscored sea
Forever unreachable, lost to my command.
I preferred the vocation, sweet, enjoined on me—
To be just where I was, and not to wander
In thought or act from work that came to hand:
To care for, cure my plots of native land
And find, in cloistered clearings, the green fields
Of Elysium, redeemed from distant shores.

Meanwhile, my vision frequented its stores;
A seer perhaps too enamored of sight itself,
Of the play of dappled shade on indolent limbs,
I cherished not only pristine things, self-sealed,
Forever turning into themselves, rapt spheres,
But the charged, immaculate spaces between them,
Like the silence between words, its reticence,
The vibrant precondition of utterance
Or of its meanings, multiple yet coherent
Though intangible as a temple's atmosphere.
I sought an art, a life, composed, intact.
I never longed to pierce, or to be pierced

(Whether by Eros or by some warrior's arrow),
To strike beyond surfaces to the pith within,
Or to be stricken, like some wounded deer,
Or if I yearned to, was balked by an urgent fear
Somehow instilled in me from my first years.

No mere poet, after all, but a latent priest,
Clairvoyant in the simplest of senses,
My vision clear, my body modest, chaste,
I only wanted to gaze, no, never to taste.
And that is why my boys were drawn to me
Or to my songs (I almost thought them the same).
They knew that I would seek, ask nothing of them,
Unlike their parents, lovers, girlfriends, wives,
And so they submitted to my words' designs
And lay about me, innocent, undefended,
Not thinking, for a time, of martial feats,
Of training in their unconquerable phalanx
That melded all, incorporate, in one body,
A soldered file of soldiers, arm in arm,
A single faultless wall of brazen armor
Deployed to repel the brashest of attacks,
To shield their polis from all threat of harm
(The antitheses of Maenads' swarming packs,
Each feeling herself the sole spouse of her god,
Each reveling, proud, in all the others lacked).

But now, lost in my song's untended moment,
The willing captives of its yielding spell,
They laid their shining shields upon the grass,
Reclined, half-shut their softly lidded eyes.
Why, they seemed almost, almost feminine
And I, a mere poet, was their trusted captain,

Confederate in the arts of peace, not war.
I gazed on their rapt features like a lover
Who wakens first, and finds the face beside him
More lovely still in sleep's unvexed repose,
And felt the aching tenderness of a mother,
A vigilance more poignant than any dream.
Still cradling my lyre, I felt its subtle humming
Along my nerves, converging on my heart
From which, redoubled, then sent forth again,
It found its way into my burgeoning song;
Its words, though uttered singly, were blended
Like drops of water vanishing in a stream.
Perhaps I was not so different from my boys;
Well, I of the lyre, they of the heavy bow—
We both were masters of the tense, plucked string.

Nearby, in sacred groves, nymphs tended wells
Reflecting, in blue rings, unblemished skies,
Bright faces flashing in a liquid mirror
At which they gazed, their stray, cascading curls,
Submerged, half-hid, in mind's clear element
Unstirred by any ripple, its glass intact,
Its oases surrounded, screened by stately oaks
From any zephyr or stiff, sudden wind;
Those stillest pools were fed by buried springs
Whose urgent sources' bursting syllables
The nymphs alone, devoted, trembling, heard
Leaping like light beneath the placid pane,
Their tones too deep for my famed lyre to delve,
Their fleeting, abiding thrum enlivening earth;
O, they were beatified by their constant care,
So comely the satyrs, mortals, highest gods
Profaned, by force, a grace none could possess—
  A brute fate that had never threatened me.

It is true I shunned the company of women,
But I was still a youth. None would suspect
The thrill of pained perplexity felt within me,
Despite myself, despite my clear intentions,
Like an arrow fixed yet twisting in my heart,
A keenest wound half blessing and half curse,
Exhilaration strangely mixed with shame.
How could I speak what yet had no known name?
I scarcely knew what it was I felt myself,
Only that what now awakened in deep recesses,
Its echoes sealed in the caverns of the mind,
Was somehow dangerous, a dark foreboding
That cast first shadows on my lambent days.

Well, after all, I was my father's son.
Bright Lord of the bow, the lyre, of dire wounds
That he alone, great healer, had skill to cure
With his scented herbs, his compound remedies.
Sadly, when he himself was cruelly stricken
With love of a youth by his swift discus slain,
He found no sure recourse to redress his pain,
Only the red-streaked flower he renamed
For his beloved, inscribing each petal "AI, AI,"
His distress unmollified by that silent cry,
Yet duly commemorated, then duly mourned;
A god, he dilated to full strength, moved on,
Returned to his high station, the resonant sky,
Resigned his staff to Asklepios; his roving eye,
Undimmed, again surveyed his broad domain.

But I was left to burn with an inward smart
He would not or could not see, a world apart—
I'd always known I was far from his chief care.
A desire as yet with no object, a parching fire

Kept wasting me from within. Only my lyre
Could quench its flames, and set me free to roam
In the placeless realm of sound, now my true home,
The self-forgetful trance from which I'd wake,
As always, balked and baffled, bereft, alone.

When at last I could not hide myself from myself,
I vowed never to act on any goad's prompting,
To let my life's inner stream flow out in verse
And yet flow nowhere, gathering force within
To radiate through each nerve, fiber, limb,
Growing like some vast cloud-headed tree
Until I almost glowed like my fortunate father
With his solar roar, his voice at whim's command,
His sovereign words as feared as those of Zeus,
Although he did not scruple to speak in riddles,
A sly trick I would not deign to emulate.

I had my pride. Should I have let it go?
Son of a god, should I have played the pilgrim
And slouched toward Delphi, jealous of a fate
I knew, in its ripe time, would be unfolded,
Neither a moment too early nor too late?
What need had I to ponder, parse, or study
The hermeneutics of the Pythia's hiss,
Her forked tongue always signaling both ways
At once, and so at once both right and wrong,
In retrospect ever true to her dazed throng?
Her words, whenever literal, proved a scandal—
It would take long years to rehabilitate
Her image, but she always bounced back strong.
What need had I for Dodona's fabled oak,
Its sibilant speech all rustling consonants
(Its eager priests supplied the missing vowels),

When nearer trees, far loftier, bent toward me
And keenly listened to my simpler song?
What need to read the random flight of birds?
Their veering chevrons, glorious to behold,
Spelled nothing but a flash of white and gold.

Should I, who shuddered at the sight of blood
And chafed at sanctioned rites of sacrifice,
The slaughter of the heifer, the conjugal feast,
The libations spilled for the unfeeling dead,
Have stooped to haruspication, poked about
The steaming entrails of some innocent beast,
Getting the lay of a torn and wasted land?
Let darkness bury darkness. Why invoke
Chthonic shades with charms best left unsaid?

Should I have played the initiate at Eleusis,
Have fasted, plunged in vapid thermal baths,
Have quaffed capacious draughts of unmixed wine,
Until, sufficiently weakened in mind and body,
Deemed pure enough to join a credulous mob,
I melded with its motley, licentious queue
Of slaves, priests, politicians, duped patricians
Who yearly trooped to Demeter's dreadful shrine,
There to meander, lost, in the soul's dark night,
Its labyrinthine cellars, its stifling caves,
Half-choking, gasping for a shaft of air,
Feet probing for the first step of some stair,
Ah, finally, one with all, to be ushered above
By a hierophant, a psychopomp in white,
To fiery tongues of light, to flutes' and drums'
Wild, palpating arias, spasms of delight,
To the painted props of a promised Elysium
Vouchsafed, at the end of life's false path,

To those who fell prostrate before an ear of corn,
Reaped and upraised, a bold, pneumatic phallus,
A tender idol, lovingly lopped and shorn?
No need to change one's life, to pledge reform—
Sufficient, more than sufficient, to have seen,
Surrendered, to a mystery, to stand forewarned,
To remember faithless Attis, his eunuch priests
Wailing faint praise to the mother of us all.
Humbled, should I have chosen to be reborn?

I had my pride. I should have let it go
Who dreamed myself to my sole self sufficient
Despite the pangs that roiled me from below,
Upbraiding me with my own mysteries,
The sprouting and hybrid flowers of my soul.
I never thought to confer with my truant father
Who never, it seemed, sought out his lonely son;
I would not plead. I would not be undone
By the chill scorn I feared he might bestow
On one who, waxing, blushed with a carnal glow
Like Hyacinth, new-veined with stripes of red,
Conceived to be cut down before his prime.
In that very fear I felt a god draw nearer,
Though even now I cannot say which one
Or if, in secret league, two gods conspired,
Only that I spied my prone, blank shadow
One morning as I strummed my serried strings
And heard, for the first time, their minor chords,
Odd tones for which I found no ready words,
Although I felt a wordless premonition
Sweep over me, untuning my shivering frame.

It was then that, suddenly, Apollo found me
(Or D dressed in my father's borrowed guise),
Enveloping me in a mist of occulted light,
And spoke the literal sentence that fixed my fate:
Henceforth, an exile, I must quit my glades,
Exchange my quiet paeans for dithyrambs,
Serve as a roving rhapsode for Dionysus,
Induce a truce throughout my father's lands
Who already shared, with D, his shrine at Delphi;
Now I would serve two masters, one command.
Impossible task! To utter my misgivings,
To tempt two gods, was dangerous and futile,
And so, mute though appalled, I bowed my head,
Resigned to follow where my ill luck led.

Tentative, I stepped from my loved clearings
Into a wood that pressed me from all sides,
Its choking thickets and its pricking brambles
Oppressing me, retarding the easy stride
By which I'd glided, free, from field to field.
Probing, recoiling, I slunk, snaking my way
On a pathless path I was bound to improvise,
And passed into a covert world of shadows
Bedazzled by glints of syncopated light;
I stroked my lyre, startled by what I played,
Its dithyrambic beat, bold, shifting shades—
By the rough new style Apollo had prophesied.

Like a tame folk singer forced to go electric
By recidivist, barbarous tastes of a New Age,
I shuddered at raw, rebarbative sound unleashed.
My lyre's amplified twang teased my ears,
Both shocked and pleased by its fresh prodigies,

But, O, the beasts my dulcet hymns once tamed,
Fretted by foreign rhythms, seized by fear,
Fled the charged bearer of a word transformed,
Now ramified far beyond its former scope—
Those intimate precincts, empty and foregone,
Were faded memories of some foreclosed era
No troubadour could recapture or prolong.

How strange to become a stranger to my kind!
The flashing forms that vanished into the brake
Left only a fleet parting, a rustling behind
Like a sudden gust of wind rippling the reeds
Of my past haunts, their recollected streams
Still voluble within me, the voice of dreams
Still whispering soothing words within my heart.

Alone and unattended, I grimly tended
Toward Ida's cliffs and caves and stately pines,
The alpine faults D made his polar home,
The hideaways from which he ranged on high,
And felt like a common trespasser. The sky
Weighed down upon me like a leaden crown.
The eagle's lair, *über alles*, the despot's eye
Olympian, freeze-framing glacial vistas,
The hygienic vaults of aesthetes on holiday,
Bare, rifted rockscapes, fetishized, sublimed,
The self its own spectacle, the ego inflated
Beyond itself, beyond mere earthly bonds,
The spirit's vertiginous whiteout uplifting all,
Wagnerian high camp shot by Riefenstahl—
All these were tricks D saved for later times.

My cold, compulsory exile was less sublime;
I secreted myself, for shelter, in a cavern

Carved, or rather gouged, in the side of a cliff,
And daily clambered down to grub for food
From grizzled shepherds driving huddled flocks
Through narrow passes, used to solitude,
Not knowing kin, communion, the only good
That I had prized, been formed by, understood,
Whose praise I sang of in my former days
To my soldiers, a listening circle in repose;
Each casual limb seemed stationed in its poise,
The body's fixed proportions a timeless truth.

Trial-tempted hero, quester, ascetic, saint,
Or forager in the woods, forced mendicant,
Were never roles that I to myself assigned
Who dreamed I played no role, instinct with self,
So seamlessly were my self and role aligned.
But now I scarcely recalled who I once was,
My frail, parched body whittled to a stick
With which to prod some jackal or rabid dog,
My soul stripped bare, emaciated, craving
Some vestige, touch of company, human care,
While shut in my cavern, O, far from oracular,
An apprentice hermit, my hermitage despair;
But I was ravaged still more by the fear
Of what I sensed awaited—D's epiphany,
For surely the God whom I was taxed to praise
By my sometime father would appeal to me,
Though in what form I dared not speculate.

I knew, from the first, my civilizing lyre
Was no match for D's redundant, vital power
That fed on itself, and yet grew ever stronger;
Though self-consumed, its own endless supply,
D's substance never wasted in the spending:

Ravenous, rampant, ecstatic, teeming life,
Absorbed, through death, still greater potency.

O, I had tidings of what transpired here
One moonless night when Bromios appeared
As sleek as a panther, pacing these same cliffs
To goad, past distraction, proud sisters of Thebes,
Impervious, who rebuffed his claimant's ire.
The moment his feet rebuked too solid ground,
Dull earth, once dormant, spun into overdrive,
Hopped up, juiced on its own amphetamines,
As Bromios pounced, himself a natural high.
Sprouting, unfolding, maturing in less than a day,
Vine tendrils hung with clusters of ripe grapes,
All fit to be burst on palates less than fine;
Fermenting instantly, rich, unmixed wine
Soon raced through matrons' overheated veins
As earth's fecundity staggered past all bounds;
Tranced nurses suckled fanged beasts, pacified
By breasts that spouted jets of copious milk
That spurted, too, from the bare pinecone heads
That tipped the lifted thyrsi firmly gripped
By Bacchae whirled in self-transcendent dance.

Hysterica passio: up, thou climbing rapture!
A thousand eager staves now rapped the ground
From which oil, honey, water, ardent, sprung,
As though from bursting wells as yet untapped.
The Maenads' leaps grew bolder, fleeter, higher,
As each assumed their deity's restless power
And trampled hard rock into the oozing mire
That stained their feet as they still blithely trod
The winepress of their odd, capricious god.

Past mania, they reeled into psychosis
Whose syntax, voiding objects, yielded signs,
Self-constellating ciphers, occult designs
So full of meaning meanings were annulled
In stunned, vertiginous, scorched, vacated minds;
Clues, portents, glancing surfaces, turning, faced
One way, to magnify the I that scanned them,
Each a rapt god in whom a god confided.
Countless glyphs with only one translation,
Like thought retraced to the mute pulse of will,
All things were Dionysus, whispered "kill,"
And in the thrilling turning of that moment
Each tender nurse waxed strong as an Amazon,
Each fiercer than a tribe of pale male hunters,
Quicker to pounce, more competent to rend
Whatever gorged beast wandered in her way,
Black widows weaving flaring, tensile nets
With which to trap, ensnare their flailing prey.
With unkempt cries they hoisted phallic thyrsi,
Shafts oozing viscous seminal milk and honey,
An orgasm prolonged past paltry spasms;
Others lit torches, dancing with forked fires
Whirled into orbits, halos round their heads
As, scaling jagged cliffs in ardent bounds,
They sought the heights of D's inchoate night;
Each dreamed herself a queen, like Penthesilea,
Would happily have severed a sagging breast
To make her aim more true, her only quest
To be a peerless hunter, rabid as Dionysus,
Ruthless to rout, uproot his implacable foes,
Usurpers of chaste rites, unsanctioned guests,
Voyeurs hot to crash their secret show.

Their fevered skin grew dark with an inner glow
As they consumed raw flesh, ah, freshly torn,
Each like black Kali, teeth begrimed with gore,
Skulls, pelts swinging from her ample belt,
Or like Durga riding bareback on her tiger,
Her mace and trident wielded by multiple arms,
Dashing worldly dreams with unworldly alarms.

O, fiercest of that whole crew was Agave,
The king's queen mother, sad sister of Semele,
A skeptic forced to yield to D's stern charms;
Her cries, pansexual, tore through the chill night,
Shrill ululations, triumphing in his will.
How suddenly she turned when his full frenzy
Torched her, rolling back her rapacious eyes,
Far-spanning, that spotted Pentheus, a bold spy,
A lion perched, incongruous, in a treetop
That she and her fervid sisterhood brought low,
Reserving for her the right to rend her spoil.
Like Perseus brandishing Medusa's head,
Poor Agave, stricken, hexed, strode into Thebes,
Vaunting the trophy of her hunter's prowess,
A lion's mane impaled on her thyrsus-spike,
Until the fit wore off, and she awakened,
To scan familiar features, broken, mangled,
Reduced to a trope, the synecdoche of her son,
Then wailed at what her bloody hands had done.

D's willing consorts, too, faced tragic ends:
Some fell in exile, others to self-slaughter;
Still others, like Agave, turned on their sons,
A compulsive, repetitive theme, scripted by D.
All were stalked by him, the stealthiest voyeur

Who, hidden, relished wracked, climactic scenes
As though he died, survived, with every one.

Pent up, constrained by close, familiar walls,
I played, replayed D's myriad thespian feats
On a tape that unwound, rewound within my mind,
Revulsion mingling with a queer attraction,
Perhaps the pull of destiny, long delayed,
Or of solitude that yearned for an encounter
That kept not happening, day by aimless day,
Each one the same, a dumb continuum,
No blessed break, the promised guest detained.
One morning as I paced, beyond distraction,
A sudden shade, cast inward, traversed my floor;
Startled, I swung around, sought out its source,
An icon staunchly stationed at my cave's mouth—
No ideal form, abstracted, no dream of reason—
Backlit by slanting rays it partly blocked—
D's dreaded, anticipated epiphany!

His mask uprose, fresh-dripping from the sea,
All head, no body, that head the height of a man,
And faced me, as others, fully frontally,
His face with a gentle smile like a bodhisattva's
That seemed to cancel all desire and fear.
But O, that smile was nothing if not deceptive,
More like the Mona Lisa's, Madonna or vampire;
Sweet monster, posed before a rocky wasteland,
Her lips, forever sealed, conceal a rictus,
A laugh whose echoes, dumb, remain congealed.
How glibly the god accosted me: I am here,
As he conjured up his visage, ex nihilo,
Challenging me to meet his steadfast gaze

As the roar of raw chaos itself assailed my ears.
I could not evade, nor apprehend obliquely—
Like Medusa's image, caught in Perseus' shield,
Seen in that mirror darkly, not face to face—
His eyes that raised me up, and laid me low;
Transfixed, my vantage was more like the Gorgon's
The moment she descried her own reflection—
O, impetuous act of self-despoiling love!—
Whose severed head toppled from its lofty perch,
As Pegasus, new born, pranced up the sky.
I felt like a soul who'd died and yet survived.
Then furtively, uncannily, D disappeared.
Plunging toward heaven, lunging into the sea,
Bipolar tropes that merged in the awful silence
Subtending the pandemonium of his reign.
How quickly all the shrilling pipes grew still,
The cymbals ceased to clash, the thunder-drums
Sank into the sanctum of the inner ear.

His mask turned inside out, turned outside in,
Was both yet neither, other to no other,
Created a space not space, a warped lacuna
Where here was always elsewhere, elsewhere here;
To gaze at him was to be displaced, unplaced,
To banish oneself completely, unless one hid,
Retreated behind his mask, saw through his eyes
Beholding the absence where one used to be.
Strange ecstasy! Not even my shadow lay
Before me, although it was far from noon,
So wholly was I consumed by his disguise.

Like a lunatic swapping places with a cipher,
I reverted to my own form, his mask vacated.
I shuddered awake, as into a further dream

Until, beside myself with joy or terror,
I once again confronted his grinning façade.
His features seemed mere copies of themselves,
The copies of a copy, themselves a copy
Of which no lost original could be found;
Reveal to me your face before you were born,
He seemed to taunt, a cruel simulacrum
Delighted to laugh at my too-earnest state.
Neither kindly master nor fierce nemesis,
He vaporized as soon as I would oppose him
And left me, lost, with nothing to impede
My headlong fall through the abyss that opened
(Within me or without—I could not tell)
Until, in the splitting of an orphaned moment,
I caught sight of his blank, unmoving eyes;
And then I was not plummeting, merely standing,
Still as a statue, balked and paralyzed,
That as by some undue miracle comes to life,
Breathes, moves, exulting in the morning air,
And feels the living sunlight gild his limbs,
A slight breeze rise and fall in his flowing hair.

At last, beside me like a lost twin brother,
I glimpsed D's human form for the first time:
O beautiful past beauty—man, woman, god,
Converging, found the zenith of their spring,
Sap rising, in his lithe and tender limbs,
All golden light, and glistening as with dew;
He smiled at me, moist eyes blue as the sky,
And in that moment, lost to all I once knew,
I felt myself his consort. Dancing for *me*,
For me alone, his sole, his chosen peer,
He deployed himself before my enchanted eyes
In gestures free and playful, hieratic and grave,

Indulgence fused with awesome majesty,
Until I was ready to tender myself his slave,
Almost, almost . . . A doubt shaded my mind:
Was this, his revelation, his cruelest disguise,
Bright unconcealment his preeminent ploy?

Quicker than thought his features reified;
A mask upreared, not smiling as before,
Its broad mouth twisted into a ludic leer,
From which a tongue, rude, lecherous, protruded,
The face of Gorgo, love transformed to fear,
The sneer of a sniggering, petulant, ancient child,
Polymorphously self-pleasuring, obscene,
Thick snakes coiling, uncoiling in her hair,
Tusks sprouting from her forehead to impale
Some crude impostor not yet turned to stone
By her petrifying need to seize, possess.

The mask was lifted. In its place a skull
Flashed fast before me, the last shreds of skin
Unpeeling from its shut, marmoreal jaws,
The concavities of its temples a searing white,
The all-color color of nothingness. I peered
Through hollow sockets that once harbored eyes
At the wide and disarticulating sky
Supersaturated, stained one immaculate hue,
Engulfing and absorbing my stupefied stare,
Until a strange vision rolled within my mind:

I saw the Ganges, torpid, dun-brown, flow,
Silted with eras of sediment, sifted earth,
Bearing, upholding all life in its drifting sway,
A goddess, gentle sustainer, slow as time.

While light grew denser with a saffron glow.
The sun swelled, softened by diffusing mist,
A pervasive, pendent, breathing atmosphere
That hovered, fed the primordial clay below.
Red-robed initiates gathered on broad banks,
Attended by priests, coiled incense. Temple bells
Told vespers from all quarters, tolling *AUM*,
The no-tone at the heart of all resonant tones;
Ascetics, pilgrims, shopkeepers, young wives
Joined with devotees—come from how far?—
Hands folded, wading waist-high in the tide
That eddied about them, currents deep, alive;
At last, drawn by the waters, they submerged
Their limp and yielding bodies. Hearts entire,
They prayed never to return to this near shore
But like the great swan *hamsa* to soar away
When spirit stole from flesh on its last day.

Fade in, fade out. My vision turned to black;
Burning ghats flared beside the flickering tide
That flashed entwining arms of tainted fire;
Smoke rose from narrow rows of funeral pyres,
A pestilent incense fogging the fetid air,
Shrouding a yellowed moon, blotting the stars.
The stench of rotting corpses, crepuscular, rank,
Clogged every nostril, sank into each pore.
Night crawlers slunk from culverts of the day,
Prostitutes, thieves, transvestites, out to play;
Vultures wheeled, then dove upon their prey.
Scavengers pledged to scare up choicest scraps,
Kapalikas followed their left-handed path,
Skeletal, brandishing their skull-crowned staffs,
Haunting cremation grounds, begging for alms;

Having taken the hero's vow, their solemn oath,
In obeisance to Lord Shiva, their all in all,
Trained to behold in all the indifferent same,
To find nothing repulsive, nothing to disclaim,
Nothing polluted, impure, but words of blame,
All things His body, all acts His gleeful play,
Sworn to slay each reflex or instinct of shame
That binds, as fast as desire, soul to flesh,
Zealous ascetics, they performed their rites,
Their foul black mass in Shiva's holy name;

And so, triumphant, conquering all distaste,
They swilled their sallow wine from cranial cups,
Devoured strips, charred ashes, of human flesh,
And thus, they thought, consumed the god himself,
Then swelled as if infused with Shiva's power
But lost themselves. Did even their god disdain
Their sacramental logic, pure, deranged?

Zagreus, too, was torn, slain, and consumed
By Titans, rebellious, antinomian crew,
Who gorged on him, yet left his beating heart
From which great Zeus, industrious, refashioned
A selfsame form to clothe the god, reborn;
Meanwhile, one bolt reduced the giants to ashes,
Their shades dispatched to blackest Tartarus,
But from their charred remains he molded man,
Gross flesh redeemed by a trace Dionysian.

How easily D subverted me from within,
His cinema unreeled on the screen of my brain
(Quick cuts, dissolves, abortive scenes, surreal)
Although all appeared to haunt me from without.

O, far from my lyre, outmoded, taming him,
My mind by his unstopped force was colonized,
Became a blank zone where lurid pictures bred,
Bright simulacra, virtual, undimensioned,
All words, all finer tones, chased from a head
Benumbed by D, his ideologue's sick designs,
A tyrant still, though I was no common slave.

His smile, smug, mock-triumphal, taunted me
One final time before his mask dissolved,
Returned to the sourceless source to which it fled,
Or joined my father, perhaps, for a tête-à-tête,
While I with my shaken sanity conspired
To find some way to drive my thoughts away
From the utter disintegration threatening them,
Decompensation, in some shrink's cold phrase,
A word with which no soul should make amends
When *fathomless horror* would serve as well,
Existence itself a soundless, empty shell.

My long exile was over. No interdict
Could bar me from my green, my native fields;
What prison could be worse than to waste here,
What penalty more dispiriting, more severe?
And so, for one last time, I cursed the cliffs
That had lately been my inhospitable home,
And then descended. The way down was easy
Compared to my forced ascent, a fruitless errand,
A slave's obedience, the extorted, false assent
Of a son whom his own father had betrayed,
Had orphaned for his own equivocal gain,
No gain at all. I sensed the price of my rebellion,
But, mad for home, discounted every cost.

Ah, finally I happened on the field I'd lost;
I knew it by its great oaks, its winding streams,
But no boys lingered there. Where had they gone?
No doubt they missed my lyre's notes, missed *me*,
And so, once again, I plucked its tensile strings.
But not one single soul appeared to greet me
And even tame beasts crouched wary in their lairs,
All wind died down, and eerie silence reigned;
It seemed my world had frozen, globed in crystal
That no clear note could crack, no zephyr thaw,
More adamant than stone tablets of the law,
Until, again, some least branch, silent, stirred,
Although accompanied by no human word.

I waited. Days. Yet nothing, nothing changed;
My lyre grew still. It had no power to soothe me
When my black moods, imperious, came on.
In every shifting shade I sensed some end,
Some inconceivable end, toward which I tended
And which, at the same time, inclined toward me,
Stalking me just past the margins of my fear
Soon to be crossed: a monstrosity almost here
Was waiting, as I waited, to pounce on me.
Only having come *home* could I be so estranged
From what I once felt, remembered, of myself,
An inner exile banished from my own source,
My solitude more sere than in the mountains
For which I almost pined, but no turn backward
Could unthink thoughts increasingly deranged
Or ravel threads that time kept playing out,
Would play out to their frayed, discordant ends
As *worse* drove on from *worsening* to the *worst*.

The mind is its own place? Well, not entirely.
I'd become, as sophists say, *the contested site*
Of irreconcilable forces that now controlled me,
Converging from without, emergent within,
The self, self-scandalized, traduced, undone,
A gutted field, a text ripped, shredded, burned;
The strings of a lyre vandalized and slashed;
Half-finished figures cut from a shattered loom,
Meaning shorn of context, orphaned, misplaced,
Its butchered fabric dangling severed threads;
Disembodied echoes sealed in an empty room;
An effigy formed of straw stuffed in a tomb;
Bare substance, uncreated, poor, forked thing
From which—as something *else*—I was reborn,
Divorced from the plighted life I dreamed I led,
Blank legend that my name no longer named,
As insubstantial, lost, as the absent wind
That still refused to rustle through my glades.

It started: a sound at the margin of the woods
That startled me, the first clear sound I'd heard
For days, the crackling portent of no good.
Robed, stately matrons stepped forth one by one
Into my clearing, eyes glazed, hypnotized,
Their motions measured, forced into no dance,
The grave antithesis of Maenads' frenzy.
All seemed the embodied soul of premeditation
Like the mute chorus of some wordless play
That unfolds toward its preordained fatality
As they strode toward me, and as I retreated,
Already ruined, to the Hebron's tufted banks,
My beloved rippling stream, too swift to cross.

O, what took place there had already happened
And I was its locus, torn by the premonition
Of my crouching form surrounded by a swarm
Of furious, grappling hands now grasping me—
I knew them well. Impossible to fight them;
I had long since, in truth, given up the ghost
Of Orpheus, had long since been impaled,
Nailed to the canceled horizon of what I was,
Collapsed to a famished point, a deadened star.

Forgive me. I have no heart to enumerate
The exquisite, painful stations of my slaughter,
To glibly parse my parts' savage dispersal;
I have no heart at all, quite literally. I recall
We poets are nothing if not literal. Forgive me
If I spare all the brute *AI* of my ruptured cries—
There are some things to be unsaid for modesty.
Suffice it to say: I should have died, did not;
No, I was entombed alive in my severed head,
Now blind, left to deduce the scattered body
Upon which my kind beasts voraciously fed—
Yet none exhumed the offal of my brain.
No kindly god reassembled my broken parts,
No penitent mother, no son (I never had one),
And my lost boys, embroiled in foreign wars,
Had passed beyond my pacifying compass;
They never knew me. They were never mine,
Were loaned me to abandon me in their prime
While I declined to depths beneath their ken.

My dark, post-mortal life, compared to D's,
Was a travesty, a sham, though Dionysian,
As if he were living his queerest role through me,
Enacting some mad, delighted self-parody,

While the phantom body that my brain filled in
Throbbed with a tearing pain entirely real.
Its wounds, though cauterized, would never heal;
Regrets, redundant, carved grooves in my mind,
A circuit, closed, enclosed in a calcified sphere
That neither light nor sound could penetrate,
The silent rasp of my prayers all I could hear,
The stuttered blandishments of a blinded seer.

O, nightmarish *life-in-death* and *death-in-life*—
Of which one later singer had heart to tell
Who became the mute Orpheus of his inner hell,
Though he at least was granted the grace to die,
His obsessive perseverations thereby stilled,
Distilled into the notes some remember him by—
You grant me no respite. I cannot wake and die
But eddy on like the Hebron in which my top
Was tossed like refuse by some bloodied hand.

I commanded myself: let *I* now stand for *head*,
Shorthand for the part still left of me, its pith
More corporeal, more real, than my abstract *self,*
A concept depleted of all its inherited wealth.
So henceforth shall it be. Thus I decreed it
Who had no further power to set the terms,
The rules for the misrule by which I was led,
Misled, launched on my false pilgrimage
Toward nowhere I had the knowledge to predict;
By rights my syntax, too, might have been mangled,
Though I was left, small solace, the gift of speech,
Yet yielded no audience for my protestations—
Which, had it assembled, would have spurned them
As if each tender ear were plugged with wax.

Besides, my father had trained me to be *meek*.
And so, no swan, I was borne swiftly onward
Past the spoiled precincts of my erstwhile dreams,
Its flattened fields, its indifferent flora, fauna,
Which I had no further privilege to see;
At last the gentle Hebron's mouth disgorged me
Into the world-circling, wild, unpastured sea.

Lone ark stalled on the dark, mercurial tides,
Orphaned, vouchsafed no second of my kind,
My pitchy head had become *un bateau ivre*,
Although, both bark and passenger, stone sober,
I had the will to command, but no possible way;
I was tendered no tiller and lacked any hand
With which to stay the waves' tempestuous sway,
Unlikely protagonist of the night sea journey,
My tests an *archetypal* phase of *the hero's quest*—
For what? *Reintegration? Salvation?* I forget.
My chaotic peregrinations spelled no end
And I, cast against type, was no Aryan hero;
I had never served as coxswain for the Argo,
Its manly crew, and my lyre's steady measure
Had never synchronized swift, thrusting oars—
A myth, like that of Eurydice, sadly untrue.

No, I had always distrusted the sea's livid flux,
D's rude dominion, soused with its own excesses,
Its ubiquitous, overlapping crests and troughs,
The hyperactive slough of my deep despond.
My head, as if set in some subtle gyroscope,
Kept turning right-side-up, facing a sky
That remained occult, an absolute zero to me,
Sunless, starless; night, day, space, and time
All merged with the lateral drift of my anomie;

Distance, direction, duration, all were unmeasured
As the looping thoughts in my untethered brain,
Feedback reinforcing the same vexed question—
Who, if not I, was the author of my fate?—
Until, keeping nothing straight, I fell to raving;
The froth about my mouth was not my own
But might have been, my mind was so far gone.

Misogynist? No. Another myth. I'd never
Loathed women, only felt drawn to my kind;
A few chaste hours spent with innocent boys—
Had they forced gentle matrons from their looms,
Impelled them to such squalid handiwork,
Provoked from them a vengeance so unkind?
Implausible, if not goaded by D's whip,
But the solemn, stately troop that had assailed me
Had revealed no trace of the Maenads' frenzy,
Had displayed, in fact, an Apollonian poise.
Could my father have rescinded his gift of life,
Jealous of the lyre he had bequeathed me,
Its seductive influence breeching mortal bounds?
The archer, impartial judge, flayed Marsyas alive
For daring, fool, to challenge him in song—
But, diffident, I had never been one to boast.
Could D have silenced me for *seeing too much,*
My stalkers' steady gait his ingenious hoax?
Could Apollo, D, have broken my body's bread,
Small price to effectuate some solemn truce?
Why taunt me, then, with mock-immortal life?
Was it I, my emergent desire, that stalked itself?
O, these and cognate questions embroiled my mind,
Unanswerable and never to be answered,
While, floundering on the self-besotted flood,
I bathed as if in my warm, spilling blood.

Between thoughts I was rapped, a sudden thud;
My miniscule ship had foundered on some shore,
A coconut fetched up far from its native palm—
O, moment of blessed stasis, just before
I was solemnly raised by massing, votive hands
Far kinder than those that last manhandled me.
A *miracle! A sign! A talking head!* All hung
And murmured, rapt, around my sunken visage
That the sun, the sea, had caulked to a stiff mask.
I petitioned for my life—for them to end it!
None paid the slightest heed to what I prayed;
No, they had other plans, those silken maids,
And in solemn procession paced to Apollo's shrine
Where I was potted, enthroned, a sacred plant
Attended, with care, by a Lesbian hierophant,
High priestess of the island to which I'd come.

Was this, then, sweet Elysium? No, pure hell,
For them a blessed isle, but accursed to me,
Though from my gentle captors none could tell
That to be irreparably stopped and stranded here,
At the polar, uttermost outpost of my fate,
Was worse than to brave the maelstrom of the sea.
I knew there was no evading their intention
To domesticate me, prized like a sullen child
Whose least, precocious squawk presages genius,
While laying me, like a tyrant's corpse, in state,
A rank flame guttering, filming my blank eyes—
Tortures too clever for Hades himself to devise.

Lord, how I yearned for D's forced ecstasies,
To morph my vestal Nereids to frantic Maenads,
For his flickering, lurid cinema of derangement
To flash, again, on my mind's vacated screen,

But now a permanent blackout locked my brain,
One life, one death, cold solitude, one fixed frame,
No savior to spring me from the sacred gaol
Where I lay sequestered with my secret shame,
No name to cry out, except, in vain, my own—
Famed Orpheus tamed, reduced to an oracle!

Ah, to be less than human, and yet deemed more!
A monster, an unholy terror, yet duly installed
In their innermost sanctum, holiest of holies,
Rescued, yet damned to terminal self-interment,
Outcast, yet smuggled within tall temple walls,
My unique debasement prompting my elevation,
My cruel election a boon to my credulous hosts,
My fractured existence a riddle to stump the Sphinx—
From me the barest fact was its own disguise.

An impotent Pan encamped amid coy nymphs
(More willing, but to no end, than doomed Syrinx),
I had no instrument but my severed windpipe,
My grating voice forced through a hollow straw,
No voice, but a hoarse hiss, a ghastly whisper,
The last recourse allowed me by godly decree.
My lyre, my precious lyre. Where had it gone?
Down Hebron, swept to the sea's imagined floor
To consort with Morpheus on his ebony bed
While I scratched forth the noise within my head.
Perhaps I dreamed I *spoke*, but merely *mouthed,*
Like a hooked fish, an agonized pantomime;
If so, the gods' joke, tasteless, was on me;
But clearly my keen auditors thought they *heard.*

My every word of complaint, however banal,
Was gold coin new-issued from Apollo's mint,

Its figures, tortured, conformed to grand designs
Far loftier than their progenitor had in mind,
Whose only intent, quite literal, was to die—
No mystical dark night, but extinction itself;
To be burned, packed in an urn, stuck on a shelf,
To annul my fool's charade, my cancelled self
Upon which counterfeit idols could be stamped
Was all I begged for with confounded cries.

My words fell not on deaf, but distant ears;
The more I repeated myself, the less they heard,
Until I vowed, hellbent, to stop making sense,
And spewed a gurgling stream of consciousness,
A wild glossolalia, post-Babel, a polyglot brew
My priestess copied, coopted, sanitized,
Reframed into the corpus of Orpheus' Hymns,
Inspiring the vulgar cult of Thrice-Born D,
Yet another crude, world-despoiling, mystery
Ensuring all comers eternal incumbency.
                                    And I
(O, crowning irony!) was named its founder.

Like "The Wandering Jew," yet unable to wander,
Immortally harried, yet hammered in place,
An internal alien, foundling, the ward of no state
But my own, but my own, my stammering dreams
Congealed to unsoundable howls of disgrace,
Self-enclosed O's, frozen shocks of brute fear
I suffered my scrupulous nymphs not to hear;
How I longed to relapse into sod, to dissolve,
Atavistic, in primal muck, stamped by no gods.

My jaws a gaping *yoni*, my tongue a *lingam*,
My face a gaping death mask, more obscene

Than any Gorgon's, fixed in an abject grin—
Like Lear, reduced to a zero without a figure,
I, memberless hermaphrodite, blinkered seer,
Was laved by obsessive ritual ablutions,
Pure torture to me, to my vestals a fond chore;
Yet still I endured, not hoping past all hope,
My vatic mouth washed out with votive soap.

Where was the boy within me, his firm trust
Displaced by the taste of terminal disgust?
Of him above all I dared not think to think
And of his harmonious numbers, so wholly slain
Not even a plangent trace of their ardor remained
To reverberate through that golden atmosphere
In which all objects rounded to their prime.
What of his verdant precincts, ripening glades?
Did no virtuous youth remember he had gone?

From time to time I heard D's truant laughter,
Far off, yet in the vault of my echoing mind,
Amid sophomoric quips (no man is an island)—
Mocking me, exiled from my body's mainland—
Or insinuating tropes (you are not who you are)
Disposable rhetoric, costing its speaker nothing
Yet leaving me destitute as a bartered son.

My graven tablets, forged in Apollo's temple,
Bore the clear, hard marks of his imprimatur
By which, at least tacitly, he legitimized D
Whose rage, in turn, was tamped, if not contained—
A pact, improbable, sealed at my sad expense.
Now neither god put stock in my spent voice
That had outlived its mandate. Had it had one?

My father, staunch upholder of the law,
Swooped down and stuck a lead bit in my craw—
While still, through later voices, I babble on,
None willing, at last, to shrive me, empty me.

So many words have been forced into my mouth:
Elegies, lyrics, soliloquies, sonnets enthralled
By noble panegyrics, proud poets' skilled
Self-flattery tricked out in my borrowed guise,
Their heads bay-crowned, my cruel fate falsified,
My ruptured flesh, my seasonless inner hell,
Atrocity's garbled shame, obscenity's syntax,
Smoothed out in rolling numbers, tolling rhymes,
All forcing me to bear glib hymns of praise:
O, Orpheus; O, *tall tree in the ear*—from which,
Bent low, dismasted, unmanned, cut down,
I, too, like luckless Pentheus, was uncrowned.

Enough! Enough sublime, stentorian lines;
It is time, past time: I refuse to ventriloquize,
Charge all to heed the ultimate reprimand
That brave Apollo poured in my stopped ears:
Even now can you not curb your wagging tongue?

For God's sake, turn away, let me be silent;
I suffer blank, unspeakable, tractless days,
Each pinned to the ruined pediment of no future
As pain sifts through my brain as through a sieve—
O, sleepless nightmare, truth wracked past belief!

Quit me, now, *be quiet*--and dream that you live.

III

---❖---

Via Dolorosa

The road changes / The road does not change.
Rough patches appear, are patched,
Or are left to grow still rougher, annoyances
That crop up along the appointed way.

Weeds force themselves in dark green clusters
Through roadside asphalt and gravel,
Marginalia no scholar condescends to read.
A driver, bored, stares straight ahead.

The commuter sallies forth, then returns.
Were he to keep on going he would
No longer be a commuter but something else—
A nomad, a vagabond, a fugitive.

The road does not change / The road changes.
Is it possible that we have lost our way?
If so, it is not the fault of our unimpeachable
GPS's, which are neutral, unaware of us.

The road, it seems, is no respecter of persons,
Like the law, with her blindfold and scales.
Though none of us, to our knowledge, are felons
Fleeing the scene of some crime.

And what of our knowledge? Does all depend
Upon our always partial point of view,
Or is it as fixed as the sky, which beholds us,
Albeit blindly, from its station above?

The road changes / The road does not change.
It must be spring. Bright yellow flowers
Push through the loam. Back yards, reviving,
Flash by us, their images glimpsed

In our rearview mirrors. The seasons change
And do not change. Yet the weather
Is different, as various as two colors we call
The same, but that can never be the same.

Unprecedented events continue to happen
If only you know how to look. Remember—
Those of us too preoccupied to be curious
Can scarcely hope to be surprised.

The road does not change / The road changes.
Somehow, without my conscious consent
A decision has been made, although I alone
Could have made it. I must have been

Distracted, elsewhere, at that crucial moment,
Perhaps in a stupor, perhaps blinded by rage;
I had had enough, was no longer willing nor able
To be a Sisyphus without a mountain.

And so henceforth would be simply continuing.
Not commuting. Foregoing my daily bread,
My kinship with others, I kept reconnoitering
New terrain much like the old.

The road changes / The road does not change.
I used to think change sponsored freedom.
If only my sober Suburban were a drunken boat—
A skiff, a coracle, a shallop, a sloop—

The ground giving way to an undulant ocean,
Monotony banished by peril and chance!
But no, I am landlocked, confined to one route,
Like fellow travelers I can no longer see.

I alone drive my car. I am dying of loneliness
Out here in what has become a desert.
I would turn back but home, too, is deserted,
Its body as skeletal as a rickshaw's.

The road does not change / The road changes.
Some of us are fated to remain as if in exile
Though exactly why and from what none can say;
Our parched throats utter no words.

Nomads. Vagabonds. Pilgrims. Yet even for us
There are moments of unexpected clarity.
Our guilt, a sentence we pass on ourselves,
Can be suspended if never revoked.

Nearby a scrap of paper flutters gracefully—
Like that scene from *American Beauty*—
In a breeze that gathers above a parking lot.
But no, it is outside of our line of sight.

The road changes / The road does not change.
Always, at noon, the sand shimmers.
Time seems to stand still. It seems too early
To be the middle of the day. I imagine

I am holding fine grains of sand in my hand.
Sifting through them, I am surprised
By how different each appears, as though
Deposited here in successive epochs

Forming different strata. Time, on a scale
Too vast to comprehend, is buried here.
The sun, already past its apogee, descends
Toward the perfect line of the horizon.

The road does not change / The road changes.
Out here there is no trace of history.
It is leached by the desert from the desert
Or from the desert by the desert.

Whichever way, it could not matter less.
The Spanish broke the Indian nations,
Plundered their land, proffered them a cross
In exchange for their suffering.

Traces persist in towns, on reservations.
But here what passes for narrative
Is the apparition of motels, then truck stops,
Truck stops, then motels. Whichever way.

The road changes / The road does not change.
My mind, in obsessive loops, recreates
All it once had, all it has carelessly abandoned,
But sadly cannot abandon itself.

Out here the air is so thick you can almost see
Its wavering eddies. Tumbleweeds,
Like the ghosts of some unknown substance,
Dance on the limitless sands of no shore.

I wonder, what must it be like to surrender
To the vagaries of the wind, to a force,
Invisible, whose motions are entirely random,
Each instant unique and unrepeatable.

The road does not change / The road changes.
Still I exist at the border between worlds—
The emptiness within, the emptiness without,
Both abide in their own inner life.

I am not blind. The desert can become sublime,
Overwhelming the mind as surely as any
Mountain, like the Alps a tourist once traversed
Unawares, first elated, then let down.

Minimalism stakes its claim: bleached bones
Bare against sand; darting birds, tiny,
Particolored; the sentinel sun; and silence;
And the whirring hum of insects.

The road changes / The road does not change,
Out here the seasons no longer revolve.
Out here even the weather scarcely changes.
Random clouds drift by overhead.

Now and then: a gas station, brightly colored.
A single pump. A single boy attending it.
Like a painting by Edward Hopper. Materialized
From nowhere. Stations along the way.

From where has he come? Perhaps from a town
Obscured by a hill. But here there are no hills.
How very proud his parents must be of him!
Still just a boy, yet earning his keep.

The road does not change / The road changes.
A mirage before me. A mirage behind me.
And silence, silence humming like an engine,
Droning its high-pitched *AUM.*

Can it be we have been waiting all this time
For a blessed, promised epoch of grace
I imagine in a future just over the horizon
But which might already have passed?

There must be some simple chapel up ahead,
Fashioned as we are, out of clay,
With an image of Our Mother, kind, forgiving,
Who will hear my cries, witness my tears.

The road changes / The road does not change.
Perhaps all along it has been leading me
To You. Already I begin to see Your features,
Your gentlest eyes, Your hint of a smile.

O Mother, I never, never meant to turn from you,
But Father said: You have to mean not to.
I never entirely embraced his negative theology,
But now it seems I am my father's son.

How often I have made decisions by refusing
To make decisions, until to act at all
Has come to seem impossible, and refusal
Has become my only gesture or word.

The road does not change / The road changes.
The day grows late, though not yet dark.
Cacti, ancient sentinels, cast lengthening shadows
That keep sliding, portending no good.

I fear that the great Refuser is now resident
In my heart, and I, a mere collaborator
In his reign of terror, have become an unruly child
Whose only delight is in saying no.

How often have I, the maddest of judges,
Both indicted and recused myself.
To whom, then, should I plead for absolution—
I, who still long to hear my own name.

The road changes / The road does not change.
As always, I have my self and its shadow
For comrades. The worst possible company,
Their words taste bitter and stale.

Perhaps my father was right to warn me of sins
Of omission. Seeming to cause nothing,
They become loopholes, portals through which
Unimaginable consequences flood.

Unable to sleep, exhausted beyond exhaustion,
I am immured, entombed in a body
That refuses to oblige me, to give up its ghost.
My afflictions are chronic, not terminal.

The road does not change / The road changes.
The desert remains indifferent to itself,
So invariant that it almost lulls me to sleep,
Then jolts me awake with hallucinations.

The body changes. The mind resists the change.
Surely my old age should be happening
To someone else, anyone else, not to me.
Eroded by my final vocation, I can see

Its degrading depredations. In my dashboard
Mirror, an effigy stares at an effigy.
Better to fix my eyes on the interminable road
From which I am too timid to swerve.

The road changes / The road does not change.
What have I learned or unlearned?
What wisdom have I bequeathed to others?
What advantage accrued to myself?

If only you keep going you will reach the shore;
You will exult as the sun sets on the sea—
An emblem, a moment once cherished by me
Back when I had moments I could prize.

What if, defying all odds, I finally arrived there
And gamboled, an ancient child, in the waves?
That destiny, thank God, will fail to manifest;
That travesty I need not abide.

Once I dreamed of the day when the same,
Yet utterly changed, I might boldly arise
Into a world all light, and there be reunited
In a final, sweet recognition scene

With all whom I have lost along the way;
My life spread before me like a diorama—
Here you were courageous. There you faltered—
A student again, I would make amends.

But now I fear I will be abruptly translated
Into a realm, a bardo much like this one,
And will be met by my double, my dim shadow
Who will ignore me and turn away.

The road changes / The road does not change.
Many travelled it before, and will again.
And I know I will end before it does, although
Exactly when, it is not for me to say.

As for you, hypothetical reader, let my words,
Though barely legible, stand as signs, caveats
Posted, for those able to see, along the way--
And may you not be led astray.

The Frame

The tops of the trees stream
As though through a denser element
But slower than in real time,
In the tempo of departure, of mourning.

And you, on your back,
Look up at them through high glass
As a familiar sensation returns,
The beginning of an elegy without words.

You lie at the threshold
Of sleep with no talent for sleeping
But with an instinct, instead,
For receding into the current of attention,

Impersonal, that disowns you
Even as it works through you to no end;
Its joy subsists without you.
You are baptized in absence instead.

Still, how exquisite it is,
That tethered rushing of silver green
Rampant against a cloudless sky-—
A vision the light frames to know itself by.

You cannot remember the day
You first stepped from the frame. Not even
The current can carry you back.
And yet now as always you cannot forget

The fate of the earliest witness
Still borne within you from time out of mind—
The sensation of seeing too clearly,
The desolate knowledge of not being seen.